The New Copywriting Paradigm:
Why Are The Stories People Tell… The Secret To Selling Them, *Anything?*

By Mark Pescetti

[Introduction]

What if I told you, **Everything you know about advertising… is wrong?** Would you believe me? And what if I also told you that MOST of what you think you "know" about advertising has virtually nothing to do with what it <u>genuinely</u> takes to <u>connect</u> with people… to sell them, *anything?*

Would you believe me, or call bullshit?

My name is Mark Pescetti. I'm an advertising copywriter by trade. I've made multiple people and companies… millions. And I did it without ever once "learning" anything about copywriting. As in, I never once read a copywriting or marketing book from beginning to end. I didn't want someone else's experience and insights to become my own.

Nope, I'm a wandering spirit by nature; a student of life, and ALL of its emotion. And my "School of Wandering" served me well. You see, I deliberately set out, at only 10 years old, as a homeless kid on Maui to discover WHAT makes people connect with me, and HOW I can sell them, anything, so I could survive... and help my mom.

Yes, as a 10-year-old homeless kid.

I quickly observed and discovered how certain words, signs, and symbols circumvented people's logic, or the "storytelling" part of their brain, and gave me instant power to lead ANY conversation where I wanted it to go. I got so good at figuring out what made people stop, talk with me, and buy whatever I wanted to sell them... that it became second nature.

But funny enough, it wasn't until 4 years ago that I discovered there's a name for how I capture people's attention... connect with them... and sell them... whatever I had to sell at that moment.

The method I instinctively tapped into is called Heuristic Psychology. And in this eBook and program, I'm going to shine a light on how you can use this simple "storytelling bias." I want you to always clearly hear and see...where people want and need YOUR help the most.

And how you can EASILY solve those problems, for them, with YOUR product or service; whatever solution you're passionate about getting in front of people who absolutely need it.

One thing:

Everything you're about to read, hear, and discover is stuff I taught myself. I didn't "learn" it. I discovered it. For myself. And that's why I'm able to predictably develop a sales campaign (by using a highly-precise strategy). I'm not guessing. I have an incredible, deconstructable method... that works in selling any product or service... to any market or audience.

So, if you're interested in discovering what marketing and advertising REALLY IS, "flip the page," and let's get this party started. However, I will say, if you simply want to discover how to easily connect with anyone, in real life, for whatever reason you want, THIS ebook is going to change your life. And I say that with a straight face. Because it absolutely did for me.

But ultimately, this project, for me, is about helping YOU discover financial and time freedom. So, while this ebook is all about marketing and advertising, it's also about how to connect with anyone to achieve YOUR dreams and fantasies. And LIVING those dreams and fantasies is ALWAYS on the other side of connection.

Which means, no matter what, you should constantly be striving for connection... in every conversation you have... or want to have. And in this ebook, you'll discover exactly how I do it, and how you WILL do it, too.

Chapter 1: Heuristic Copywriting

Everyone is telling a story. It's the ONE THING that unites and connects all of us, no matter where you're from, what religion you do or don't resonate with, or what language you speak; we ALL "talk" the language of story.

And when you truly understand that; when you truly GET that everything in advertising... starts... and ends... with the STORY your prospects are telling...

You can look at any product or service, and know exactly how to position it, to either join, or interrupt, the STORY your prospects are collectively telling. Of course, HOW you position your offer means everything. You MUST successfully join or interrupt the story your future customers or clients are telling to earn their attention. I'm talking about the problems you can authentically solve with your product or service.

And we're going to cover every aspect of that fact, from the inside out, and the outside in.

Now, it's important to know where I'm coming from. Any origin story has its breadcrumbs. So, how did I organically discover Heuristics as a homeless 10-year-old - who sold tropical fruit on the side of the road in Maui's Iao Valley? After all, I'm NOT traditionally educated. In fact, I dropped out of school in the fourth grade for health reasons.

Long story short, my mom moved my brother and me to Maui to start an "alternative healing retreat." The problem was, the day we got there, my brother, who was fucked up on meth freaked out the owner of the healing retreat property my mom had contracted with. And after just one night on the property, he broke the contract.

In that moment, we went from living an upper-middle-class lifestyle... to becoming homeless... literally overnight. My mom wasn't the smartest business woman. She left her family, *us*, with a mere $500.

Now, I was still recovering from being sick. That's why I was originally pulled out of school. I felt fragile, alone, afraid, and not sure if I was going to be okay. I saw the look on my mom's face when this all happened. I knew it was real. And I knew there wasn't going to be a hero coming to our rescue.

That fact became more real the very next night. We were driving around looking for a place to sleep and arrived in The Iao Valley on a humid, rainy night. My mom shacked up with the manager of the Iao Valley Lodge, while my brother and I slept outside. He had a tent. I didn't. I was left to figure out where I was going to sleep, in the jungle, with no blanket, pillow, or anything to cover me. I was never so scared in my entire life. I walked most of the night, in the jungle, by myself, crying my eyes out. I needed someone to tell me, **"Everything's gonna be okay."** But there wasn't anyone there to tell me.

I was alone. So alone that if I had died that night, nobody would have even known where to find the body. I grew up a lot that night. It was one of those defining moments when I could have broken. But for some reason, I didn't break. I fell asleep as the sun was coming up, lying alongside the Bloody River. In that moment, I found my okayness. I discovered how to feel "home"... on the inside.

Sure, it was just a flicker of a feeling, but it was a very real knowing inside of me. And every day since then, I've nurtured the knowing that I'm home, and complete, within myself. While scary, it was also the most empowering experience of my life. I woke up about three hours later... and I didn't feel so alone.

I woke up with something I had never felt before:

The absence of fear. The knowing it was my own Natural State to feel whole and complete, without anyone else "giving it" to me. I also knew that things were different. And I could either resist the change... or I'd just create more pain. So I decided to embrace the adventure, and let go of everything I thought was... real.

But something else miraculous happened. As I was sitting on a boulder in the river, eating some starfruit, I noticed hundreds of trees around me. They were heavy with mangos, papayas, coconuts, bananas, passion fruit... and tons more starfruit.

I asked myself:

"What if I could harvest and sell that fruit? I bet people would flock to give a 10-year-old homeless boy some money... for amazing tropical fruit."

So the next day, I approached the manager of the Iao Valley Lodge about doing just that. I even offered to give him a cut. I quickly got approval, and he didn't want a cut. I mean, he was already sleeping with my mother, and gave her shelter, while I wandered in the jungle, getting poured on all night.

But something magical happened that day. It was something far more important than the horrible circumstances I was facing; I became a salesperson.

And my endless journey of constantly watching and observing people, their body language, their choices, and their energy... became my classroom.

And in the process...

I discovered the #1 way to sell or share anything:

Through storytelling.

Join me as I unravel the strange world of advertising. I'm reveal how to easily position ANY product or service to become profitable... by simply understanding how to join or interrupt the story... your audience is telling.

Plus, you'll discover why the mechanism of a campaign is infinitely more important than your hook or big idea. Truth be told, without the mechanism... you can't break through people's heuristic defenses. Because unfortunately, whether the story your prospects are telling is what they want or not... they're going to protect that story... like their lives depend on it. And unless you have a foolproof mechanism to break through that story, you ain't selling shit!

Join me in understanding how all of this craziness works, and HOW you can sell or share anything... by simply knowing the story your audience is telling.

Chapter 2: Why Story? Why Heuristics?

Before humans even had verbal language, we had story. Before we had Facebook, we had cave drawings. And absolutely nothing has changed; stories are still how we communicate. And our storytelling abilities have only been harnessed exponentially with Social Media... and the internet in general. Because now, stories get shared and perpetuated at the speed of cellular data.

With that in mind, **let me ask you a question:**

What's usually the very first thing you do after something dramatic happens in your life? You usually tell someone about it, right? Because sharing what's happening in our lives is how we communicate... and connect.

And get this:

The majority of "stories" that people communicate are rooted in fear, scarcity, and negativity.

Here's why:

Human beings are equipped with a physiological AND psychological defense mechanism called Negative Bias.

It's a built-in "feature" in our Autonomic Nervous System. And it FORCES us to constantly scan... for problems. And for MOST people, they're painfully TRAPPED in the Negative Bias Cycle. In other words, they're constantly telling stories about what's wrong what COULD happen... and how they're poorly treated by virtually everyone in their lives.

Here's the fundamental truth about advertising:

Nobody gives a flying @#$! about what you have to say - until you emotionally connect with them, first. You have to provide everyone who sees your campaign with ample chance to "see themselves" in the story YOU'RE telling.

Your prospects have to instantly believe, **"YES! You're talking to ME".** Because even if you're selling the HOLY GRAIL... nobody cares. And they won't care, until you connect with their pain and fears. Again, Negative Bias FORCES us to focus on the bad stuff in our lives.

The point is, you likely won't develop a scalable advertising campaign (that'll produce passive income for a long, LONG time) unless you clearly KNOW the "story" your avatar is telling. And then you have to figure out how to get your avatar's attention, *quickly. This requires* effective positioning... backed by a clear mechanism... to join... or interrupt... the conversation your prospects are telling themselves… about the problem your product addresses. A mouthful, I know.

I discovered this as that 10-year-old homeless kid watching the people around me compound their pain by getting lost in **the negative story** they were telling. I knew they were SCREAMING for help. But nobody could get my mom or anyone else around me to raise their hands. Nothing ever connected with them, and so they remained in their mediocre, poor, homeless, scarcity-minded prison cells.

That's what happens when real, authentic solutions never get to see the light of day… nobody ever gets help. **That's what advertising is all about:** Helping people. And helping them "see themselves" in your marketing message. So, if you're not taking the time to understand the heuristics or the story your avatar is telling about the problem you can help solve, mountains don't get moved. You'll likely never have a viral, iconic, immensely profitable campaign that stands the test of time.

So, always remember:

The more people you help, the more money you make. But it always starts with asking the right questions that get people raising their hands. And that right there is WHY I got into advertising… and WHY I'm writing this ebook. Because more people, than ever, are telling horrible stories about their health, finances, relationships, and more. These stories are causing them massive emotional, physical, and even spiritual pain.

As advertisers; as marketers; as visionaries, it's OUR job to emotionally connect and inspire these suffering people with REAL solutions. Again, that's WHY I'm writing this ebook. I want to help you connect with the people you want to HELP. And I can clearly PROVE HOW my method converts on cold traffic in ANY market or niche. I can also PROVE WHY Heuristic Copywriting is one of the most effective ways to HELP people, connect with them, and get them to purchase the REAL solutions…

That can change their lives. That's the power of advertising. Unfortunately, it's a power that's rarely exercised in this Wild West advertising world. Because way too many people IN marketing are just chasing the money. They aren't asking themselves, **"How can I HELP these people, who are so obviously suffering, with my authentic solution?"** It's a disease. And it's spreading faster than Donald Trump's infectious brand of arrogant ignorance.

The good news is, Heuristic Copywriting can INSTANTLY separate you, your product, your service… and MAKE your campaign JUMP out from the sea of bullshit.

And it always comes down to ONE THING:

What story is my audience telling... and how can I connect with it? At the same time, I'm using my unique positioning and mechanism strategies as a way to bridge people's problems with the valuable solution we're sharing with them. I'll do a deep dive of how I come up with the right positioning, and mechanism, later in this ebook.

Quick disclaimer:

I didn't "learn" that stories sell; it was just something I naturally did. I *knew* I needed to make a connection with people before they were ever going to buy my fruit

Or accept my offer to show them around "the cool spots" in the Iao Valley of West Maui as a 10-year-old homeless kid. And I very, very quickly realized that desperately trying to get people's attention so my family and I could eat wasn't the answer.

I knew that on an instinctive level. Again, until you make an emotional connection with your prospects, they DON'T care about what you're offering them, no matter WHY you THINK they SHOULD care. Read that last sentence again.

And I tried... or tested... countless ways to attract customers to my little roadside stand that the manager of the Iao Valley Lodge allowed me to set up. I wrote different messages on my signage every day to see what did or didn't work. Then, when people would stop at my stand, I'd immediately walk up to them, and frame my body close to theirs. I wanted them to feel my vulnerability.

Now, when they'd ask me questions about the fruit, since I didn't know anything about them, except for their flavors, I'd talk about HOW I got them. If they asked about the starfruit, I'd tell them a story about the Menehune village I found, right near all the starfruit trees. And inevitably, I always sold lots and lots of fruit to virtually everyone who stopped. My conversions were through the roof.

I knew I discovered the path of least resistance to connect with people and sell them… anything. That's the power of story; the power of Heuristics. But WHY does storytelling work? We'll explore that… next.

Chapter 3: Can You *See* Me Now?

"We thought that we had the answers, it was the questions we had wrong." —U2

So, I discovered, very early on, that relating with people made me feel grounded, calm, and relaxed; connection gave me the sense that, *"I'm NOT alone. It's okay. Everything's okay."*

Relatability and connection made me feel home. And because of that, I found myself constantly developing my abilities to build rapport and lead conversations. I discovered that, if you listen closely, people are always telling you their story. They're telling you what their problems are, as well as what they believe is (and isn't) possible… for them. Ultimately, people are always revealing where their biggest pain points and triggers are.

Hell, people will even transparently tell you, with absolute passion where IN their story your potential customers or clients are hiding their biggest pains. Because it's all they talk about! It's all about listening and asking the right questions (which I'll talk more about in a minute).

Now, have you heard the term *Mentalist* before?

According to a simple Google search, being a Mentalist also means you're a magician. But a "true" Mentalist will tell you it's not magic or psychology. That's not really how Mentalists observe, connect, and communicate with people. In fact, as someone who considers himself a true Mentalist, this real-life superpower ilis less about listening to words, and more about listening to my own empathy.

Now, empathy is always going to play a HUGE role in your life. Always has. Always will. In other words, you're constantly feeling empathy. It instantaneously and simultaneously affects you, and the people you're connected with, without beginning... or end.

Truth be told, you're empathetically "talking" to people all of the time. It's an invisible stream of REAL communication that speaks to you, speaks through you. Oftentimes, empathy can overwhelm you, because it makes you FEEL so fucking much. That's why most people try to shut it down, usually at a very young age.

Maybe you don't even resonate with what I'm saying, because you did try to turn off your empathy. And now feel disconnected from it. But it's there. You DO have it. It's that annoying voice in the back of your head, or that gut feeling that tends to conflict with what you "know".

You know what I'm talking about, right? The stuff you "learn" through standardized education, religion, spirituality, and your upbringing in general.

But what exactly is it that GIVES you, that gives us this supernatural... superpower?

Two words:

Mirror Neurons.

Now, I "accidentally" discovered Mirror Neurons when I was just 5 years old. At 5 years old, I went into my mom's bedroom and found a Betamax copy of the movie *Rocky*. It was the first adult movie I watched from beginning to end. I won't lie, I couldn't turn away from the TV.

I was instantly hooked from the first scene at the Bucket of Blood, where Rocky beat Spider Rico. For some weird reason, I SAW MYSELF in the Rocky Balboa character, story, and his underdog journey. His emotions were my emotions. His neurons firing became my neurons firing. And that is, in a nutshell, what Mirror Neurons are. Neurons firing, not based on your first-hand experience, but on someone else's physical or emotional experience.

That's Empathy.

It was such an empowering experience. It was like I got hit over the head, with this invasive but positive knowing that there is this supernatural ability inside of me. And this empathy connects me with the outside world. From that day forward, I lived my life from the basis of my empathy. As a fourth grade dropout, observing, listening to, and responding to my own empathy became how I interacted with the world around me.

Empathy taught me everything I "know."

In fact, I never once read a copywriting, marketing, or advertising book. I get every tidbit of information I will ever need by nurturing, and staying connected with my own empathy.

Now, remember when I said empathy has always and will always play a role in your life? Well, it does. Every day. All day. Even in your dreams. You wouldn't be interested in sex… Without Mirror Neurons. You wouldn't be a college or professional sports nerd who has massive team pride… Without Mirror Neurons. You wouldn't want to give your kids everything you never had… Without Mirror Neurons. You wouldn't even give a @!%# about love…Without Mirror Neurons.

Are you beginning to FEEL their importance? I mean, can you SEE me now?

Mirror Neurons are what **create the feeling of importance and consequence** in everything you say or do. So when people tell me, ***"I'm not very empathetic..."*** I worry. Because we live in a world where empathy and how you naturally connect with the world around you aren't what's nurtured in our society; knowledge is. And yet, it's *the truest information* you will ever have access to.

So…

As a copywriter…

As a marketer…

As an advertiser…

As a solution alchemist…

As a Mentalist…

The most important skill I can possibly have and nurture is paying attention to my natural empathy. That's HOW you can easily connect with and SEE people's stories. That's WHY I'm able to write and position offers, in any space, on ice-cold traffic, and convert like crazy. I know how to connect with people's pain points and easily lead them (i.e. new customers).

I do it all through an evidence-based mechanism. It's the bridge between the problem…. and your solution; the product or service that provides reprieve from their problems. Pretty cool, right?

For instance, I worked on a project that included developing the actual supplements they wanted to sell. I had to come up with the *One Thing/One Thing*, also known as *Their Problem/Your solution*. That's the very essence of writing Direct Response Copy. Going into the project, all I knew was that my clients, my partners wanted to target the deeper causes of weight gain. So we can give our customers a REAL weight loss solution.

During my first collaboration call with the clients, I pitched going after gut health as the basis of the campaign. Gut-related campaigns are doing really well on cold traffic, and I able to isolate some pretty awesome science to back up our claims. Then my researcher and I found two specific strains of bacteria: one that evidence shows can make people gain weight, and one that's shown to help people lose weight.

Here's how I first riffed to enter the conversation:

"What if I told you that losing weight, getting healthier, and feeling happier…

Isn't so much about YOU…

But a very specific kind of "alien" bacteria that uses YOUR body…

As their host?"

I went on in the third page:

"And get this:

Even though you may not know it yet…

As strange as it sounds...

You're 90% non-human.

And only 10%, well... you.

So whose health are you really trying to maintain…

If YOU want to lose weight, achieve a toned, sexy body…

And feel younger… and more vital than you did…

Even in your 20s?

You guessed it:

The good bacteria.

And here's the honest reality:

If you aren't supporting your army of good guys...

It's basically letting the bad guys...

Win."

Do you see the mechanism? Do you see the One Thing/One Thing? Oh, and it's coming from a doctor's voice, which is massively important. I'll explain why a little later.

But what's really important to get from this chapter is:

How I'm entering the story or conversation, which is **Positioning 101**.

Here's the thing:

You CAN'T position your copy, campaign, solution(s), and brand, without a clear mechanism that bridges your ideal customers problems with your specific solution. You simply won't trigger people's Mirror Neurons. You won't HELP your customers. And you won't profit a dime. In other words, being a copywriter; being an advertiser is less about selling the actual product or service and more about delivering a message that emotionally connects. You have to immediately inspire people to engage, believe, and buy. And it's 100% about triggering people's Mirror Neurons.

That being said…

Let me give you a hint about how to apply this stuff:

It's never about you. It's never about how much money you think you should make from a promo, commercial, or campaign. Nope. Instead, it's about imagining, from an empathetic place, what YOU would feel going through very negative, and very specific circumstances.

This goes way beyond the cliché of, *"Putting yourself in your customer's shoes."* Nah, this is about diving into your own empathy so intensely that you're almost living the circumstances yourself. And you can't help but need a solution just as bad as your ideal customers and clients do.

From there, your Mirror Neurons are activated. You can begin to mentally, emotionally, and empathetically process HOW to enter or disrupt the story your prospects are telling. That's HOW you HELP people. That's HOW you can inspire prospects to connect with you, your solution, and your brand, and become lifelong customers.

By the way, you can totally ask the wrong questions, just as I quoted at the beginning of this:

"We thought that we had the answers, it was the questions we had wrong."

And I'm bringing this up, because even if you develop a campaign you think will CRUSH IT… ***"Because it's so @#$%&! good."*** You have to make sure you are asking the right questions, *first*. And while you might have copy that sings, and production that looks frickin' Hollywood; if it doesn't **connect with your prospects**, they simply won't care. And if they don't care, your prospects won't become customers or clients.

But now, you're starting to get how you can easily avoid ever making that mistake again by focusing on empathetically connecting with people. Because rather than "hooking prospects" with something catchy (and completely void of substance), you can now truly connect with them, and keep them engaged… until they buy. That's what Mirror Neurons do. And that is how you help people.

Chapter 4: Okay, I Know What You're Thinking…

Okay, okay, I know what you're thinking:

"How do I get MY prospect's Mirror Neurons to turn on… so I can turn total strangers… into lifetime customers?"

After all, that's what it all comes down to, right? Well, to turn on, or activate, someone's Mirror Neurons, they need a trigger, something to relate to or identify with.

What do I mean?

Ask yourself:

"What grabs my attention… and won't let go?"

In other words, what triggers your story? What triggers your memories? What triggers your deepest, most honest desires?

What do YOU feel when you're broke, broken, sick, in fear, and hopeless? Do you look at successful entrepreneurs and imagine enjoying the freedom they have?

What do YOU feel when you're looking for love and companionship? Do you look at someone you find attractive… and see the two of you being intimate and building a life together?

What do YOU feel when you're lost… and need help to LIVE your passion and purpose? Do you fear the worst… and need someone to remind you of how capable you REALLY are?

So the question is:

"How the fuck do I trigger those emotions, instantly, in my prospects… so I CAN lead them to my solution?"

The answer is simple:

Describe the circumstances your prospects are collectively feeling, right now, and figure out how to get them to SEE THEMSELVES in the emotion you're describing. For instance, I did this in an online video presentation for a successful, anti-aging facial serum:

"Your eyes are one of the BIGGEST indicators of your age and attractiveness.

But they often lie.

Deep wrinkles, expression lines, crow's feet and the dreaded under-eye puffiness...

Make you look 5, 10...

And sometimes even 20 years OLDER than your REAL age.

It's genuinely NOT fair.

And it's a problem that BILLIONS of people deal with...

Around the world.

So you're definitely not alone.

But let me ask you an important question:

If you could EASILY turn back the clock...

As much as 20 years on your appearance...

Using a brand new ingredient...

Would you want it?

And if you could <u>literally erase</u> those unflattering expression lines, wrinkles, and puffy bags from underneath your eyes...

In just 90 seconds...

Like this:

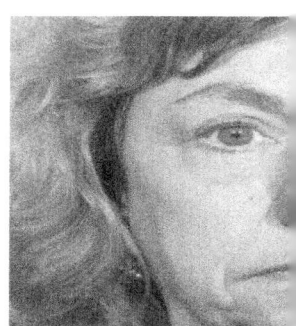

Would you do it?

Hi, I'm Dr. Shuba Dharmana.

I'm a renowned Cosmetologist & Dermatologist."

Now, there's a lot to unpack in the lede... or script opening.

For one, I had to immediately tap into one of the STORIES... that women with expression wrinkles... tell themselves.

So I said:

"Your eyes are one of the BIGGEST indicators of your age and attractiveness.

But they often lie.

Deep wrinkles, expression lines, crow's feet and the dreaded under eye puffiness...

Make you look 5, 10...

And sometimes even 20 years OLDER than your REAL age."

And it rang true for prospects. I know that, because it converted really well on Google Display and made a lot of money until the campaign was stopped for being scaled too quickly by the media my client/partner hired. Next, I wanted to take that pain and give them a reprieve from the story they're collectively telling:

"It's genuinely NOT fair.

And it's a problem that BILLIONS of people deal with...

Around the world.

So you're definitely not alone."

This triggers a serotonin response, like you get when someone holds you, and says, ***"Everything will be okay."*** This establishes that prospects CAN feel differently about the story they've been telling, even if it's incredibly brief. Next, I wanted to interrupt the current story prospects are likely telling:

"But let me ask you an important question:

If you could EASILY turn back the clock…

As much as 20 years on your appearance…

Using a brand new ingredient…

Would you want it?"

This plants the subtle seed that their problem isn't actually a huge deal. Next, I need to add proof. Because I just made a big claim. And if I don't immediately substantiate it, people will quickly start coming up with objections.

So I said:

"And if you could <u>literally erase</u> those unflattering expression lines, wrinkles, and puffy bags from underneath your eyes…

In just 90 seconds...

Like this:

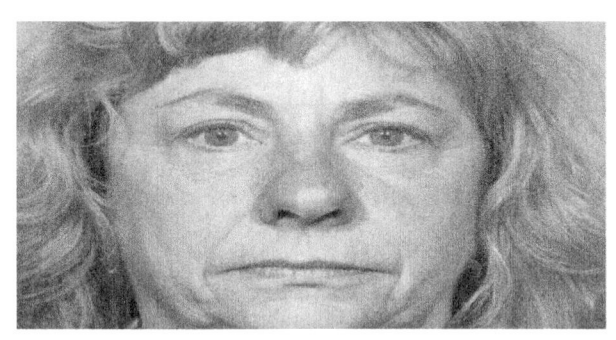

Would you do it?"

But there's a problem.

Because unless these words are coming from a credible face and voice...

It's just plain hard to believe.

So I immediately solve that:

Hi, I'm Dr. Shuba Dharmana.

I'm a renowned Cosmetologist & Dermatologist."

Because a doctor's voice makes the most sense from a heuristic or storytelling perspective. And anything less will make prospects lose faith, fast. In a sense, you have to tap DEEP into people's subconscious minds. Because truthfully, most people aren't even aware of WHY they created the problems they have, much less HOW.

They just want a solution.

That's why stuff like the direct response advertising cliché of, *"It's not your fault"* works so well. You can't make people responsible for something that they aren't really conscious of creating in the first place. Your job is to give them that instant sense of, *"Somebody sees me. Maybe they have a solution."* And that connection; that reprieve you've just given this total stranger… AKA, your new prospect… can buy you a few seconds to KEEP their engagement.

Notice I said a few seconds, because that's the truth.

One line of copy…

Only exists…

To get prospects to the next line.

Which means, you gotta know how to continuously trigger people's Mirror Neurons, every step, or every line of the way, until you LET them buy. And I say "let", because that's how much anticipation should be built up in your prospect's bodies at the chemical level. Just like initiating sizzling foreplay between two lovers before having sex.

Now, here's the truth about most people:

They aren't interested in fixing something that isn't broken. For instance, most people don't invest in preventative medicine. Instead, they pay really good money to fix a problem. Because before illness arises, there aren't any emotional triggers to force them to tap into their story and motivate them to ACT.

So when there isn't a specific problem to get underneath people's skin, first, you CAN'T get their attention. It's virtually impossible. That's why going after people's pain points is *infinitely* more effective than targeting or future-pacing their desires. No, that doesn't mean you shouldn't target their desires, also. Of course you should! But people won't listen to what you think they need or want… until you connect with them… where they are... In the story they're telling…right now.

But don't worry, I know it seems like a lot to consider and kind of a daunting task. But to make it way easier to implement, I've developed an incredibly effective copy structure to follow in Video Sales Letter (VSL) scripts, sales letters, webinars, commercials, upsells, and just about anything else. My exclusive method makes tapping into people's stories and keeping their attention… simple.

No, not easy. But very, very, VERY simple.

Here's what I mean:

Writing any kind of advertising promo has a natural unfolding. Just like any good story has a natural unfolding. I saw myself in the Rocky Balboa character, because I got to follow his journey from the beginning to the end. The movie producers were able to captivate my attention *through my emotions*, which allowed them to tell the entirety of their story, without me turning off the TV, or walking away.

The story Sylvester Stallone wanted to tell had so many specific circumstances that triggered the SAME or similar emotions I felt. It kept me engaged for the whole two hours and two minutes.

So, let me ask you another question:

How do YOU naturally absorb information? How do YOU naturally learn new things? Is it more effective for a professor to teach you something? Or… is it more effective for you to intuitively learn something new by relating to a well told story, involving the same kinds of emotions and circumstances that you deal with?

Does seeing that character go through their journey make you SEE YOURSELF in the very story that's being told? You see, when you emotionally connect with a story or narrative, their problems are your problems, their breakthroughs are your breakthroughs. Their triumphs are your triumphs. And beauty of it all is… and how this all comes back to advertising… Is that their answers… can become your answers.

Their solutions can become your solutions. And when you offer prospects the chance to take action… on an offer that can potentially change their fate, action is a natural, and highly likely, next step (AKA, hitting the BUY button). Are you beginning to see why Heuristic Copywriting works in any market or niche?

Good. Let's keep going. And, by the way, heuristics can be summed up like this:

Emotion/Circumstance.

In other words, for every emotion you target, there's a circumstance that brings it to life. Consider the example of the wrinkle serum, emotion = insecurity, circumstance = eye wrinkles. And the reverse works just as well: For every circumstance your prospects are dealing with, there's an emotion you can target to help people FEEL the STORY you're tapping into (in their psyche).

And again, it works, because we're ALL telling a story. And when you can get people to raise their hands to a specific emotion or circumstance, and they identify with the framing of your words, prospects are infinitely more likely to become your lifetime customers. But in order create lifetime customers, you have to check yourself, and your intentions, *first.*

Chapter 5: How Can I Help You?

So, there's an epidemic in digital marketing:

Greed.

The reason?

"It's so easy to make money online - if you know how to manipulate people."

And it's true:

You absolutely *can* sell people a shitty product, by positioning the offer *just right*, allowing you to manipulate the shit outta people, and make a killing doing it. After all, big brand companies have been doing it through ads in Life Magazine, TV, newspapers, and radio for years. But now, with the internet, any Joe Blow can have the same ability to get a message in front of people to sell them their "solution."

Because… get this:

Product developers, service providers, and entrepreneurs are all telling a story, too. They're telling the story about investing the least amount of money to achieve the biggest return on their investment. And unfortunately, we, the consumers, are the ones who get screwed. I'd even go so far as to say that more advertisers are probably ripping off their customers than there are companies and individuals selling authentic, original, and extremely valuable solutions.

And if you fit into the first category, close this ebook on your phone or tablet… or whatever you're reading this on… and never open it again. I can't help you - if you feel good about ripping people off.

………………….

Still here? Good. Because without value, none of this is information really applicable. In other words, it takes real, authentic value to tell a story…that interrupts or joins…the story your potential customers are telling… right now. Besides, how do you, as the person selling something, feel about putting worthless offers in front of people? And how does putting a worthless offer or solution in front of people give you the inspiration and insights necessary to ask the right questions, so you can HELP people, and nurture them, all the way to the buy button?

It doesn't.

That's why, I have a saying:

"The more people you help, the more money you make."

And it's 100% true. It's 100% compliant with the traffic platforms, and it's also a 100% scalable way to build a campaign and make sure it's producing profits… every single year. On the flip side, a campaign driven by greed is WAY more likely to bomb. It'll run its usual, pathetic course, until eventually the promo dies a miserable death (after a fairly predictable amount of time).

But why?

Why do the profits end?

Simple.

You didn't provide any value. And if you did, you didn't communicate it in a way that connected with people's STORY. And if there's no value… or no empathy in your messaging, people's stories won't change and they will NEVER become lifetime customers.

Ultimately, it's getting people to use the product, and actually getting them to tell a *new story* about it that builds your brand and increases profitability over the life of your campaign.

So, with that in mind, let me ask you a really important question:

Why are you in business? In other words, what's YOUR WHY? And here's WHY... knowing your WHY... is so important:

I always say, *"It's not <u>what</u> you do; it's <u>how</u> you do it."* In other words, the way you approach looking at something determines what you'll SEE, what you'll believe, and how you'll respond. Or in your case, as someone who wants to share and sell something, it's about caring enough to tap into your own empathy. Yes, YOUR empathy. You have to discover how to find your way into the problem your prospects NEED you to help them solve. That's how empathetically connected you should always want to be, so you CAN ask the questions that get prospects to raise their hands, and validate your desire to help (with their purchases).

That's the mindset portion for HOW you develop a winning campaign. Like I said previously, it's about asking the RIGHT questions to find your mechanism, hook, messaging, and positioning. But the tragic truth is, you won't find the right questions... if you're chasing the money. You'll simply miss asking the questions that allow you to truly NAIL the pain points, and truest desires, your audience feels, and wants.

In other words, you have to remove your marketer's hat, and put on your regular human being eyeglasses on. Which means, in order to think like a marketer, you have to live your life, feel everything as much as you can, and REALLY observe your own empathy. You have to constantly do this to the fullest extent of your abilities; FEEL as much as you can.

That's some of the most authentic market research you have, and will ever have access to. And that leads me to another question:

When YOU have a problem, how do YOU like being talked to?

Or, let me ask it like this:

How do YOU feel when you KNOW you're being marketed to, and you feel spoken down to, like you're an ignorant, little child? I mean, we're told to talk or write at a 5th grade level, right? But does appealing to a 5th grader mean you need to hit them over the head with one marketing cliché after the other? Or, can you truly advocate for your prospects, and give them tremendous value, just by watching your "free video presentation?"

The answer is not only, yes, **but a resounding "YES!"**. Because just pushing a solution or offer in front of someone, without asking the right questions, and showing that you actually care will never give you an evergreen campaign or funnel. Not one that stands the test of time.

Because that's what an empathetic campaign does:

It emotionally connects with people's pain points and desires in timeless ways. And that's what Heuristics does; it emotionally connects with the deeper, archetypal truths behind the emotion you're describing. But again...YOU... have to come from the most empathetic mindset you can find within yourself, first. That's literally how you can engage and draw prospects in long enough to become raving, committed, lifetime customers.

Now, I've personally been through a lot. And I grew way beyond the confines of conventional living or even conventional wisdom. And it's actually my lack of standardized education, and conventional upbringing, that made me the copywriter I am today.

I didn't have regurgitated nonsense and lies shoved down my throat like the majority of humanity has to put up with. In fact, there wasn't even anyone there when I was a kid to tell me, **"What I couldn't do."** Which was one of <u>the biggest favors</u> my peers *never gave me*.

I also discovered that when you really listen to people, all they're doing is telling you what they believe *is and isn't*... possible... for them. All they're doing is projecting their shit onto you. But more than that, people are always revealing to you that they need help. In fact, if you truly begin to pay attention to the stories people are telling, you'll quickly discover what areas of their life they're <u>screaming for help</u>... the most.

Which makes the following question the biggest question in this ebook... so far:

<u>Are you listening?!?!</u>

Because it's knowing how to identify and hear how people naturally and emotionally yell, kick and scream for help. But it's subtle. It's with their words, their body language, and the deeply embedded STORY they're telling. And beginning to recognize, decipher, and truly understand the deep emotional needs of your potential customers gives you the biggest insights into HOW to connect with their problems...

And lead them to YOUR solution.

But why? WHY does this stuff work so well, and so predictably? Well, not only is there an answer, but the answer will give you even deeper insights into how you can intentionally connect with people's very identity and connect them to their NEW story directly through your copy. (Like I just did, right now;-)

Chapter 6: A Look Under The Hood (Why does advertising work?)

Why do you want, *anything?* Why do you crave a specific kind of ice cream? Why do you want a particular man or woman? Why do you imagine yourself having more money? More freedom? More love? More happiness? And more life to live?

Well, it all comes down to one word: Chemicals. We are ALL drug addicts. And the biggest culprit of them all is, Dopamine; the chemical behind our virtually all of our desires. You. Me. And everyone. Are dopamine addicts. This chemical is the reason certain drugs… like cocaine… are so addictive id, they increase dopamine. It's that *special little chemical* that FORCES you to want stuff… from people… to money… to freedom… to things. Strangely, dopamine is also the same happy chemical that makes you feel rewarded.

Funny side note, men's dopamine plummets just BEFORE orgasm when they're masturbating or having sex. It's the promise of the orgasm that drives men. And well, advertising and consumerism is the same; it's the drive for more… for something better. And it's always wanting something better that constantly triggers the dopamine response in men AND women.

It's a self-feeding, emotionally-based, chemical reaction that NEVER ends… until death. And if you can trigger your way into your prospects' dopamine loop, you'll instantly get underneath their skin. Because you're literally INSIDE the story they're collectively telling. So, when I say, **"Put out messaging that MAKES people raise their hands",** it's dopamine that you're ultimately targeting.

It's dopamine that MAKES prospects raise their hands; it gives you the POTENTIAL to sell them something. Because dopamine is what inspires and convinces us to do… absolutely everything. It's the motivator. And it's the reward. It's simply a matter of finding your way into this self-perpetuating, self-feeding loop… inside the STORY of your prospects.

"But how?"… right?

Now, understanding *the dopamine mechanism* is an essential part of being a good copywriter, marketer, and advertiser.

In simple terms:

Contrast = Desire = Dopamine = Action.

So, let me break this down:

When you're in the midst of experiencing what you DON'T want, like being overweight, feeling fatigued, and sick all of the time, it FORCES you to want something better. In other words, the contrast of what you don't want births new desires for what you do want. And your job, as a copywriter, is to find your way into THAT story.

Which goes back to the beginning of this ebook:

You gotta make your prospects; the people you want to help the most RAISE THEIR HANDS. It comes down to whether or not you can paint an emotionally vivid enough of a message to excite people's dopamine loop?

And how can those circumstances trigger another important chemical:

Cortisol? Now, cortisol is a powerful stress hormone. The adrenals secrete this chemical when you're faced with something stressful (or something you really don't want).

In the advertising world, leading with people's pain points is usually more effective than trying to hook prospects by describing the emotionally-driven benefits your solution offers them. In other words, most people aren't interested in your solution, or its benefits, until you tap into the stress (or the contrast) of what they don't want... *first*.

Here's the trick:

You can ask a question that triggers BOTH dopamine and cortisol at the same time. And you should, in order to have the most impactful, and highly converting copy, possible.

Now, here's how I discovered this:

When I was 9 years old, I got pulled out of the 4th grade because of disease. I'm not gonna go into the disease here. But let's just say that my days on this planet were numbered. Well, three and a half months into this nightmare...

I asked myself:

"What if I could heal?"

And that one question triggered a rush of fear; a rush of excitement that lifted me up... at the exact same time. In other words, BOTH dopamine and cortisol were simultaneously triggered just by asking myself one *simple*, "What if" question.

The point is, it was that one "What if" question that NAILED BOTH EMOTIONS; the very core of my biggest fear and my greatest desire… all at the same time. After all, it's in the space that lies in between fear and desire that's the "sweet spot" in helping people… and making potentially tons of money in advertising.

Of course, this is where asking the RIGHT questions matters the most. Because if you ask the wrong questions, you're just having a conversation with yourself. Which means, if your campaign's messaging is even slightly off, you won't convert. And you'll watch your business get unceremoniously flushed down the toilet.

The simple reality is, if you don't connect with people's stories,
At the physiological level, you won't connect with people's natural desires. So, to give you an idea of what kind of "What if" questions have worked for me, check these out:

"What if it were possible to effortlessly build your business,

And multiply your profits 10x,

With just a few <u>simple texts from your phone</u>?

Would you want it?

And what if this same solution could <u>easily replace everything you're doing</u>, right now, to digitally market your business... sell more products... or get more high-ticket clients?

Wouldn't you want it IN YOUR HANDS...

Immediately?!?!"

Now, this is a fairly simple message. And while there's a lot of hype here, I immediately provide very real proof, which gets through people's objections, before they even have them.

Here's another one example from another campaign:

"And the worst part is...

Your STORY about scarcity and limitation...

Keeps growing...

Every. Single. Day...

Constantly blocking & resisting what you DO want.

Even if you use Law of Attraction and other manifestation techniques.

But what if it could be... different?

What if there was an easy way to tap into The Field…

So you could start living the life of abundance you've been dreaming about?

What if wearing this simple pair of headphones…

For just minutes-a-day…

Could AUTOMATICALLY help you dissolve the STORY…

That's STOPPING YOU from freely accessing The Field's UNLIMITED POSSIBILITIES?"

Now, these are just a few examples, but they give you an idea about how I either framed and prefaced a solution, like I did with The Wealth Compass, or using a few very simple "What if" questions. These "What if" questions quickly hit the heart of what those prospects were stressing about and wanting. I (correctly) identified what would… most effectively… target massive dopamine release. That's what it means to get inside of someone's story.

On a side note, I'll get into the traffic side of this in a little while. Because obviously, getting the right set of eyes, or the people who have the best chance of raising their hands onto your campaign is absolutely crucial for ANY of this to work. But here's something else about asking a "What If" question. You see, "What if" questions naturally open up people's psyches to be curious and want to discover more.

So, the next lines after your "What if" questions really need to inspire trust and hope. They need to provide a slight reprieve from the problems you're agitating in your prospects. Like this follow-up to the first text-copy example:

"Hi, my name is The Dude (obviously not his real name.)

And check out these screenshots:

Campaign	Format	Price	Clicks	Conversions	Revenue
Max Synapse - Trial - US Only	CPA	$40.00	5,438	411	$16,440.00

Campaign	Format	Price	Clicks	Conversions	Revenue
Max Synapse - Trial - US Only	CPA	$40.00	5,327	401	$16,040.00

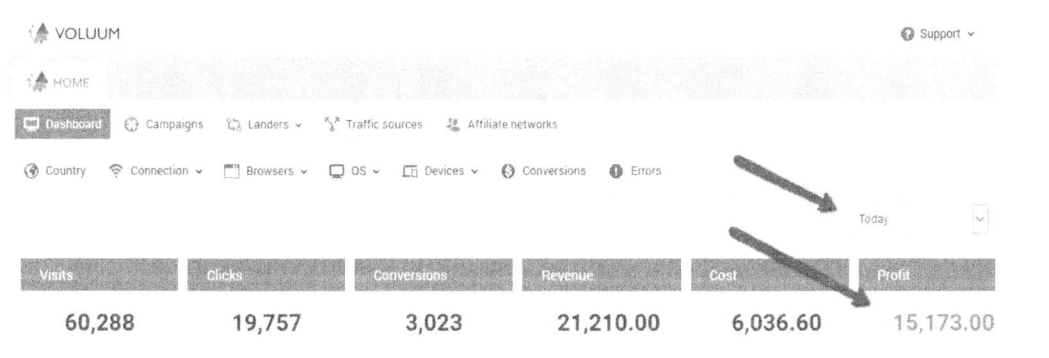

Visits	Clicks	Conversions	Revenue	Cost	Profit
60,288	19,757	3,023	21,210.00	6,036.60	15,173.00

This is how I live my life;

I profit thousands of dollars-a-day...

Without barely lifting a finger.

All because I discovered how to <u>use my cell phone</u> to ethically market my products and services via text...

Earning me 6-figures-a-month...

Without hardly even trying."

And man, even reading that myself, I think, *"That sounds so fucking hypey."* The thing is, those were actually true claims. And I later provided the mechanism behind those claims to demonstrate how ANYONE using this solution could achieve the same potential results.

But it only worked, because I triggered BOTH cortisol, and dopamine, in the initial question I asked prospects. I'll go way deeper into this process… in the video series I made to supplement this ebook, because I've only scratched the surface of how to trigger specific chemical responses in people's bodies. The questions tha inspire them into becoming lifelong customers.

However, for the sake of this chapter:

The bottom line is, everything we do; every major decision we make is born from contrast. And if you tap into people's contrast (i.e. their old story) just right, you'll easily be able to leverage their desires, until they press the buy button.

Chapter 7: The Power of Vulnerability

There are two incredible forces in the universe:

Opposition and Vulnerability. One pushes. The other pulls you in. One is very masculine, or more of a Patriarchy. The other is more feminine, or more of a Matriarchy. Now, I'm gonna go what might seem a little sideways, but please, stick with me. What I'm about to reveal is a major influence in how I write copy.

Okay, so, in Ancient Egypt, there were different eras, right? They had multiple bronze, silver, and golden ages. What's interesting is, Matriarchy was the leading consciousness, or way of thinking, during some of the biggest peaks in Ancient Egyptian times. What's even MORE interesting is, Matriarchy is NOT the opposite of Patriarchy.

In fact, Matriarchy is a perfect marriage of the masculine and feminine. In other words, Matriarchy blends opposition WITH vulnerability.

Here's what I mean:

When you blindly oppose something, because it goes against your beliefs, it only breeds more opposition from the other side. And that's a very Patriarchal cornerstone; you oppose what you disagree with, **"Because I'm right, and you're wrong."** That's just an extremely prevalent trait in the masculine psyche.

However, Matriarchy infuses the feminine, softer, more vulnerable consciousness into the Patriarchal, **"It's my way, or the highway"** hardness, and often, closed mindedness. Can you see why one way of thinking lends itself more easily to finding middle ground and invites people into a conversation, rather than shoving certain beliefs and judgements down their throat?

It's the same in advertising:

When you shove information down people's throats, you aren't connecting with them. And they bail.

That's WHY stories sell:

They share information… in a personal way… and allow people to relate and identify with it. Mirror Neurons anyone? And when you share an extremely vulnerable story, about a subject people can relate and identify with, it draws prospects in. It can't not. In other words, the Patriarchal approach tends to be condescending in "his" unwavering stance. On the flip side, the Matriarchal approach uses the same masculine strength, but does it through sharing, opening up, and asking the right questions.

Can you FEEL the difference?

Now, I "accidentally discovered" this concept on my own... during an ugly argument with my now ex-wife. We were going at it tooth and nail over moving. I wanted to leave the area where we had lived over 10 years. And she wanted to stay. It was incredibly heated, and neither one of us were showing signs of backing down. So, I took a leap, changed my tone, and expressed in a softer way, why it was so important for me to move.

The moment I stopped opposing her and opened up about why I was so emotionally charged, she instantly softened, and the rest of the conversation was beautiful. I realized, **"Wow, my vulnerability is SO powerful... that it immediately ended the opposition... and allowed us to connect... and get on the same page."**

What's funny is, I always had a naturally condescending tone in my copy, which is a BIG no-no. And it was through discovering this vulnerability that allowed me to begin to to edit out the condescending tone in my copy. I began seeing the needle moving in ALL of my campaigns by simply applying this more Matriarchal approach.

I found a balance of having a strong, authoritative tone with a softer approach, that more easily connected with prospects, and turned them into lifelong customers.

Now, ask yourself:

What EXACTLY is an emotional trigger? Well, everyone is telling a story about the issue you're trying to solve. And within that story are all kinds of specific details just waiting to be pushed against. And that's what an emotional trigger is. It's a thought process already happening inside the mind of your prospect, and all you need to do is join it or interrupt it.

In other words, connecting with the overall story... and its specific details... that your prospects are telling about the problem you solve... are HOW you enter the conversation with your promo.

So, the obvious question is:

What story are your prospects telling? And how are you going to trigger it? Well, infusing vulnerability into the tone of your campaign, or a Matriarchal approach, will almost always beat a Patriarchal strategy. Everyone wants to FEEL seen and validated. Everyone wants YOU to SEE the most raw aspects of the problems affecting them, and inspire them with a solution that erases all their past failures (to clear the deck for the purchase).

Oh, and you need to convince and persuade your prospects to feel ALL of those things (in just the few first seconds of seeing your ad or sales message). No pressure, right? But that's the power of vulnerability; it can instantly draw prospects into your messaging.

Here's the thing:

Being vulnerable in your copy doesn't mean you need a face and voice that just gushes about his or her story. Not even close. Vulnerability can be expressed in multiple ways, from compassion and empathy, to clearly expressing the problems your prospects are having. You also have to do it in a way no one else has before... so your future customers and clients *genuinely know...* they're NOT alone. You can even show vulnerability by sharing *your own* circumstances about the problem you and your prospects share... in a way only you can.

But the truth is, the power of vulnerability goes far beyond the obvious.

You see, in marketing and advertising, we're arriving in a new paradigm. And in this new paradigm, authenticity will always outsell substanceless hype. It wasn't always that way. Not even close. In fact, hype has not only been winning in the advertising world. But it has silently been destroying the heart and soul of WHAT advertising can, and should, ultimately be.

The biggest power advertising has always had is

Connecting real products and solutions with real people who genuinely want and need them. So, stop for a second.

Here's the most important question, *so far*, in this ebook:

What circumstances, in your life, can you recall where you used vulnerability to "change the conversation?" How did vulnerability open doors of communication that would never have otherwise existed?

The bottom line is, nobody got anywhere, without bumping up against HUGE challenges. And if you can find a way to showcase and highlight what those vulnerable challenges were…. And how you overcame them… You'll organically connect with, engage… and convert… MORE prospects into customers. Well, way more than any amount of pushy, Patriarchal sales hype… ever could… or has any right to.

Chapter 7: It's not you, it's me

If you haven't guessed it by now, I'm big on questions.

So, let me ask you yet another question:

How good are you at having quality, long-lasting relationships? Seriously. How good are you at reaching out, being vulnerable, clearly communicating, and constantly building your connections and rapport?

Here's why I ask:

Everything I've talked about, up until now, is all about being able to easily initiate, grow, and nurture relationships. That's what marketing and advertising, IS; it's connecting with people, and (hopefully) developing a lifetime relationship. But just like any relationship, "forever" is only possible, if you nurture it, *today*. Which means, it's not about getting something. That's not what advertising is meant to do;

It's about what you can GIVE. I know, sounds counterintuitive, right? Because the whole reason we advertise *is* for profits, right? The thing is, that's only half true.

Here's why:

Profits are the natural result of connecting with people's pain points (to help them see that you see them), providing (and clearly communicating) value, and being able to OVER-deliver.

That's WHY you always focus on helping people, rather than chasing the almighty dollar. Make sense? And how can you guarantee you OVER-deliver? Simple. Ask the right questions. Because just like any relationship, everyone wants to be seen and validated for their own personal experience.

So, what questions, allow you to ask the right questions? Good question. I'm glad you asked ;-) The answer is, as far down the rabbit hole as you MUST go to discover what makes prospects raise their hands. That's what this whole ebook is about; getting people to raise their hands, and say, **"Yes! That's me! How did you know? And how can you help me, quickly?"**

Think about it like this:

When you connect with someone for the first time, like a new lover, your whole world becomes about THAT person, doesn't it?

Well, it's the same in marketing and advertising:

When a new prospect discovers your campaign for the first time, it's like the first time you feel infatuated about somebody; It's overpowering to virtually all of your rational senses. And when you truly understand heuristics, you can hear people's stories so loud and clear. That it's almost impossible to NOT know how to connect with them to override their rational mind, and sell them what you're most passionate about getting out there.

I'll give you an example:

When my daughter was about 4 years old, I had made some really bad financial decisions. Long story short, I made my family very, very, very broke. The sad reality was, I could work for 24 hours a day, for the next 10 years, and I wouldn't have made enough money to pay off my debt, or been able to provide a good life for my family.

So, in December of '05, I went to the coffee shop everyday, up in Eugene, Oregon, and wrote a little ebook, just like this one, called, **Becoming: The Evolution of Being.** It was a spiritual ebook about how I create my own reality from the inside, out. And even though it was a frickin' grammatical mess, people loved it. That little ebook showed me what's truly possible, when you connect with people, who are looking for YOUR help.

And no, we didn't make rent come January 1st. We were 4 days late. Still pretty amazing though, when you consider it was just an off-the-wall idea. But with some Google natural listings exposure, and an embarrassing little website I taught myself how to make in a day, I was able to produce 6-figures, in just 6 months. And in over 10 years time, it made me over a million bucks.

What's even more interesting is, I NEVER had a chargeback or refund. And mind you, the ebook was just a Word Document converted in a PDF. No design. No fancy graphics. No formatting. But it was enormously well-received. What's funny is, I had no idea, until I got deep into marketing and advertising, how truly unbelievable it was to never have had a single chargeback.

What's particularly interesting is:

Up until that point, I had always kept my real story, and what I had been through in life, *hidden*. I felt like my life was too "unacceptable" or literally "unbelievable" to be real and open about. So, Becoming was the very first time I opened up, let myself be vulnerable and authentically communicated how a 4th grade, non-schooled, feral, homeless, hippie kid created his own unconditional abundance. All by myself.

It connected with a very specific kind if person, on such an intimate level, that people reached out to me right and left, expressing their gratitude. And I took major notice of this fact, which I'll dive deeper into in the next chapter. But I realized, **"Wow, I've been hiding my story… my entire life."** And yet, the first time I opened up about who I am, and what I went through, my journey towards unlimited, and often effortless abundance, truly began. And I was producing all of these sales and movement, without coming out of pocket a single penny. I discovered how to authentically put myself out there, and get people, just like me, to buy my $17 PDF/ebook from a random Google search.

Plus, I was creating all of these amazing relationships with people, I never met. And never would meet. And as I moved forward with marketing my Becoming ebook, I started bringing in 5-figures a month; something I never did before. And before I knew it, I had people approaching me about helping them market THEIR products and services. So I thought, **"Why not?!"** And took the leap.

That's when I discovered copywriting.

As I dove into copy, I realized I'd been doing it the whole time. I just didn't know it. Even now, my story has been used in marketing campaigns, like 15 Minute Manifestation, and The Wealth Compass. My story has successfully connected with perfect strangers, develop a relationship with them, and sell them my extremely valuable and effective solutions.

But here's the thing about copy:

If you DO share your story, and it doesn't emotionally resonate with the people you want to help, it's important to NOT tell a story about it. (i.e. Your "failure.") In other words, if something doesn't connect with the people you want to help, it's you, not them. So, if you "fail" to initially connect your solution with the people you're in business to help, take the hit on the chin, adjust, and start over…

By asking:

"What WILL connect with my prospects and make them raise their hands?"

Don't let NOT asking the right questions, right out of the gate, stop you from ultimately connecting with people. In fact, nothing should stop you from making a major impact in their lives, while making a butt ton of money in the process. So, if you want to discover how to find the "x-marks-the-spot" of emotional connection, and build a highly scalable, highly profitable campaign that stands the test of time, keep going, and "turn the page."

Chapter 9: The Magic of Momentum

When I was that homeless 10 year old in the Iao Valley, I sat on The Bloody River.

Here's what it looks like:

You can see the Iao Needle in the background. It's a beautiful place

It was there I had a profound revelation:

It's not a matter of creating movement, but rather, it's more about finding your way into the natural flow of movement and momentum. Maybe that doesn't quite. make sense, so here's an advertising analogy:

The essence of effective digital marketing is like finding just the right spot to enter the river. You don't want the water to be trickling downstream, nor do you want get in where it's rushing. You want to find just the right spot to get into the water.

When you're selling something...

You need to find just the right spot to "enter the conversation". This "entrance point" into the water... or conversation... is critical to the success of your entire campaign, maybe your whole business. The beauty of writing copy the way I do is, every story, every person is telling... is full of "entrance points" into the river (i.e. the various ways you can get people to raise their hands and relate to your messaging).

The question is:

What messaging and positioning are you going to use to get people's undivided attention? What symbols are you going to put in front of people, so they raise their hands, and become raving customers and fans? Because the stories people tell have MASSIVE momentum... about the problem you solve. You just need to find your way, and flow downstream... one line of copy at a time.

Now, embedded in this river flow of emotion are all different kinds of triggers (or entrance points into the conversation) to WIN their attention, and inspire prospects to realize that your solution (where the river ends) is THEIR holy grail.

That's WHAT Heuristic Copywriting IS; triggering people's emotions with identifiable and relatable symbols. And your copy is literally like the river's current. It determines how fast or slow of a "journey" your VSL script, sales letter, or webinar is - before you "let" people purchase your product or service. And here's a little secret: You need to find the "tone" and pace in your copy for people to "see themselves" in it. In other words, how close can you get to the collective story your audience is telling?

If you can successfully answer that question, it'll massively help you keep as many prospects as possible continuously flowing downstream. The thing is, everybody has different tastes for how they approach advertising, just like we all have different ways of acting in our relationships and friendships. Some of you might jump in at a point in the river *where it's roaring...* or full of acute emotional triggers. While others might find a gentler place to ease their way into the conversation, and more subtlety inspire prospects to want to keep flowing downstream.

For example:

Do you remember, **"Where's the beef?"** It was a commercial done by the fast food restaurant Wendy's. The commercial showed an old lady looking at a hamburger bun, and well, she doesn't see the meat. So, of course, she asks, **"Where's the beef?"** It was an iconic campaign. And it worked because it "entered the conversation" at a "point in the river" where the flow of momentum was strong, but not overpowering. It hit the, **"get more for your money"** pain points. But it did in a totally non-threatening way. The commercial got a lot of people to raise their hands.

Because it mirrored (as in Mirror Neurons) what a lot of people wanted:

More value for their money. Look at a commercial like, **"Where's the beef"** versus one of those Denis Leary Ford commercials that did really well. Denis Leary's voiceover always talked about heavy-duty towing capacity, while getting great fuel economy.

Like this:

https://youtu.be/dhEkVakVWFE

But it was more the tone and pacing of the messaging in the commercials that worked. Denis Leary really appealed to the hardworking "Everyman", connecting with their feelings of being overworked and underappreciated. Something very close to the hearts of Ford's customer base. Plus, the video footage and production is full of connective symbolism. And these symbols trigger the prospect's ability to relate to (or associate with) what the brand is representing (which is often the biggest pain point/desire that audience experiences/wants).

Again, it is through the triggering of Mirror Neurons that allows the audience to see themselves in YOUR advertising. So, when I personally write copy, I always try different "jumping off points". This allows to enter the conversation WHERE people are having just the right amount of emotion to pay attention to my messaging, without feeling like I'm hitting them over the head with a 2x4.

Here's another for instance:

I wrote copy for a sleep supplement. And in one approach, I entered the river at a quieter point, where the the momentum of emotion was strong, but still somewhat gentle.

And it turned out like this:

https://drive.google.com/open?id=0B-8j0cGRbrshZUg3eUNiY0xRc0k

However, I also wanted to enter the conversation at the much more emotionally charged part of the river (where the momentum was flowing hard). And as someone who also suffers from horrible sleep problems, it wasn't difficult for me to find the relatability factors that make sleeplessness… such a nightmare.

The second video turned out like this:

https://drive.google.com/open?id=0B-8j0cGRbrshdThlQUU0b0tpeTg

Can you FEEL the difference in tone? Can you SEE how I entered the conversation differently in both? So, which one, won? Well, the 2nd one KILLED the 1st one. It SUCCESSFULLY hit people's more urgent emotion, rather than trying to connect with someone who's simply trying to sleep more.

It's important to mention:

A lot of people have an issue using "hyped-out" copy to connect with people's pain points. It feels too disingenuous and snake-oil-salesman-like to them.

Two things:

1) It's NOT hype... if your marketing messaging emotionally resonates with the end customer.
2) There's a reason "positive" marketing tends to be massively outperformed by more sensationalistic, pain-addressing messaging.

And here's why:

Most people won't pay attention to you - until they BELIEVE you can help them fix a problem that FEELS like it has a lot of gravity in their lives. In other words, it's really hard to get someone interested in what you have to say - when the problem you solve doesn't have that emotionally acute, high-water-mark part of their story... you can address and help solve.

So, why did I want to try a softer tone - when there was so much more acute emotion to connect with in the story people tell about NOT sleeping? Simple. The tone I wanted to convey in the first piece was one of being nurtured, and softly supported into getting more sleep-filled nights. And if the company gave me more time, I actually think I could have gotten better results with the softer approach.

I just needed to find the emotionally-charged, high-water-point in the positive approach. And it was far easier finding the high-water-mark in the more direct, in-your-face approach. That's probably true for a great many campaigns; in both commercial and/or direct response-style marketing. It's just easier hitting the high-water-mark of emotion - where the flow of emotionally-charged-momentum is the strongest.

Of course, if you miss connecting with the high-water-mark, you're dead on arrival, and probably won't have much of a chance to rectify the campaign. And that's how some of the greatest solutions ever NOT known end up on the bottom of the sea of sameness; where products die amongst other shipwrecked campaigns.

So, not only is having an understanding of momentum in marketing, *important,* it could literally mean everything in being able to VISUALIZE where to enter the river (or enter the conversation).

Now, in a sea of questions, here's one more:

What's the #1 thing I discovered to virtually always connect with people's emotional high-water-mark, no what what the niche or market you're in? "Turn the page" and drink in my last download for connecting with people's stories, like a well-oiled machine, so you can help them, and make boatloads of profits.

Chapter 10: The constant. And the variable.

I'm always striving for one thing, in life, and in copy. And that's relevance. In fact, when I first sat down to write this ebook, my original idea for naming this project was around, *"How to become relevant in advertising."* Because that's what I've always tried to become in the advertising world, *relevant.* And what does it MEAN to be relevant?

Well, three things:

1) You're always focusing on HOW you can HELP people.
2) You're always committed to asking the right, deeper questions.
3) You're always EXCITED and INSPIRED to be on the cutting edge of innovation in your space.

Now, I'm an extremely insecure person. I have very little self-esteem. I think I look funny. I don't have a formal education. I grew up in the jungle as a feral hippie kid. I'm loud. Crass. I only have a couple of friends. I take care of my mom who has Alzheimer's Disease. I'm divorced. I have a 15-year-old daughter who doesn't talks to me anymore. I've had cancer 4 times in my life. I suffer from a horribly painful kind of Lupus. I rarely sleep through the night. I eat alone for 99% of my meals. I don't have anyone to share the holidays with. Nobody to celebrate my birthday with me. And I have never fit into society.

Because quite frankly, I spent 99% of my time growing up, from about ages 10-19, mostly by myself. I was too shy and insecure to ever reach out to people. And I didn't feel acceptable to society. I simply didn't have the tools, awareness, or experience to relate… with anyone. So I just hid myself away. But that's okay. I had experiences that in my 39 years on this planet, I've discovered, are special and rare. I discovered how to "empathetically observe." (i.e. I watched people on the outside, but paid attention to how it made ME feel, on the inside.)

I watched. I saw. And what I SAW was emotion. I saw people go through massive ranges of emotion over money, love, growth, health, spirituality, survival… and so much more. And as an adult, I've taken those experiences; those things I observed, and leveraged them to grow up. I went from being a feral hippie kid to helping people make money… through simple emotional awareness'. Sure, maybe I'm still kind of feral, but I love my wild, jungle boy side. It's a big part of who I perceive myself as being.

Yup, the Hawaiian jungles were my classroom. And I "learned" things nobody else around me had a clue about. And you know why? Well, being homeless, out-of-school, and on my own, there was nobody there to tell me *what I couldn't do.* In other words, going through the tragedy of growing up homeless and poor became THE REASON I'm one of the top copywriters in the world. I did it without ever ONCE reading a copywriting book or taking a copywriting course, too.

And after 10 years of being in the advertising business, wearing the hat of a copywriter, I've made people 8-figures, *combined.* In the process, I've discovered how to FEEL relevant. Because as a copywriter; as someone in the advertising industry, I've unearthed a powerful way to influence and inspire... the world.

Think about it:

Advertising is responsible for persuading how people think, and the decisions they make.

- The Diamond Engagement Ring
- Christmas
- Brushing your teeth

These are things we largely do, because of advertising and copywriters. Don't believe me? Well, do the research yourself.

And what you'll find when you do your research is:

The true power of advertising is to define, and redefine what's relevant. That's power. And it's a power that needs to be protected, nurtured, and ONLY used for the powers of "good." So, when I sit down to begin strategizing and positioning a new product and offer, I'm always looking for The Relevance Factor. That's why I often help develop… or redevelop… the product and ideas clients bring to me to sell.

I want to GUARANTEE I'm able to make bigger, more dramatic, TRUER claims than everyone else in the space I'm writing for.

I'll give you a for instance:

I just recently completed copy for a weight loss supplement funnel. Now, when the client came to me, they knew they wanted to enter the weight loss marketplace. But they didn't know how they wanted to do it. So, in our first collaboration call, I isolated gut-bacteria as the hook. The idea being that the human body is made up of over 90% bacterial cells, and only 10% human cells.

So, whose health are you trying to take care of - f you want to lose weight? Yours? Or the bacteria that manipulate your brain into craving all the sugary foods that make it virtually impossible to ever sustainably lose weight? Well, I went with the latter.

Here's how I entered the conversation:

"So, what if I told you that losing weight, getting healthier, and feeling happier...

Is less about what YOU do...

Or even YOUR food cravings...

Would you believe me?

And what if I also said...

Your food cravings... and emotional eating...

Are the result of non-human intelligence...

Or 'bugs'...

Living in and on you...

And manipulating your brain...

For their survival...

Would you still believe me?

Well, it's not science fiction.

These 'bugs' are real.

And the worst part is…

They're affecting every part of your life…

From the thoughts you think…

To what you ultimately eat and drink.

And the winner largely decides whether you're skinny…

Or fat;

Whether you're happy… or flat out miserable.

So, the question is:

Do you want to take back control over your body?

Or…

Are you going to continue allowing these 'bugs' to pile on the pounds…

While you deal with mysterious health symptoms that keep popping up…

Seemingly…

From 'Out of nowhere'…

And making your life miserable?"

And right there, I created a relevant conversation that's on the cutting edge of REAL-WORLD-SCIENCE. But, of course, I had to figure out how to make it actually possible. So, my team and I worked with the manufacturer that would produce the actual supplements. I want to develop a formula that would be different, and give people a brand-new weight loss option… that genuinely works.

And we did it:

We discovered a single strain of good bacteria that's supremely present in skinny people, and almost invisible in the gut's of overweight or obese people. We then combined this single strain bacteria with two extremely well studied fat-burning ingredients (that literally help fat cells, drain). It's a great front end product. And it'll help redefine the weight loss industry. That's the POWER of relevance.

But that certainly wasn't enough. Because as everyone knows, the REAL money is made in the upsell funnel. So, I had to make sure the supplements we put in front of our new customers were truly worthy of their full, undivided attention. And my team and I accomplished that, too. Upsell #1 is a 6-bottle upsell. No brainer. The 2nd upsell is a prebiotic that specifically FUELS this one good bacteria, so they can take over the gut ecosystem, and help accelerate weight loss. While the 3rd upsell targets the Biofilm that bad bacteria secret to protect themselves, and hide in, along with the natural ingredients to kill them once they're exposed.

It's a beautifully designed funnel, and its level of relevance is 100% on the effectiveness scale. Because it's on the cutting edge of where ALL weight-loss products will be focusing in the next few years. Mark my words.

Now, The Constant in advertising is:

Always asking the right questions, and diving deeper down the rabbit hole of a problem - until you arrive at a solution that takes into account ALL of the latest advancements of what's available to people. That's The Relevance Factor. The Variable is how you stylistically want to position your offer, and establish a mechanism that makes a product or service relatable and believable… to the people you want to help. That's advertising in a nutshell.

So, the bottom line out of everything you've just read (and watched) is:

Everyone is telling a story. Your job, your work is figuring out how to get the most relevant, authentically helpful solutions *possible* in front of your prospects. Then, it's your PURPOSE in life to inspire those people to raise their hands, and help them SEE THEMSELVES in your campaign.

With that in mind, the very last question I'm gonna ask is:

How are you going to put all of these pieces together in a way that emotionally connects with people instantly, establishes your credibility, and positions your offer to OWN THE ATTENTION of your ideal customer?

Much love… and good luck.

If you'd like to contact me for Copy/Business Coaching or hiring me to put together a funnel for your next launch, get at me:

Mark@reflectionmarketing.com
(541) 880-4241
Skype: markpescetti
Instagram: mark_pescetti
Facebook: http://www.facebook.com/markpescetticopywriter
Web: http://www.markpescetti.com

Printed in Great Britain
by Amazon